EXTREME MACHINES

THE WORLD'S MOST UNUSUAL MACHINES

Paloma Jae

 Raintree

Chicago, Illinois

www.heinemannraintree.com
Visit our website to find out more information about Heinemann-Raintree books.

To order:
☎ Phone 888-454-2279
💻 Visit www.heinemannraintree.com to browse our catalog and order online.

Edited by Nancy Dickmann and Megan Cotugno
Designed by Jo Hinton-Malivoire
Picture research by Tracy Cummins
Production by Victoria Fitzgerald

Printed and bound in China by CTPS

14 13 12 11 10
10 9 8 7 6 5 4 3 2 1

Library of Congress Cataloging-in-Publication Data
Jae, Paloma.
 The world's most unusual machines / Paloma Jae.
   p. cm. -- (Extreme machines)
 Includes bibliographical references and index.
 ISBN 978-1-4109-3880-0 (hc) -- ISBN 978-1-4109-3884-8 (pb) 1. Machinery--Juvenile literature. I. Title.
 TJ147.J34 2011
 629.04'6--dc22
                    2009051426

Acknowledgments
The author and publishers are grateful to the following for permission to reproduce copyright material: Alamy p. **23** (© Phil Taplin); AP Photo pp. **6** (Gareth Fuller/PA Wire), **7** (Gareth Fuller/PA Wire), **18** (HEINZ DUCKLAU), **24** (Shuji Kajiyama), **26** (Anja Niedringhaus); Corbis pp. **4** (© Roland Weihrauch/dpa), **10** (© Transtock), **11** (© Bettmann), **13** (© Reuters), **22** (© Rainer Schimm/Messe Essen/epa); Getty Images pp. **15** (STR/AFP), **16** (ChinaFotoPress/), **25** (YOSHIKAZU TSUNO/AFP), **27** (FABRICE COFFRNI/AFP); Honda pp. **8, 9**; Rinspeed Inc. pp. **17, 19** (Dingo/H. Streit/Jeebee); U.S. Navy p. **14** (Chief Petty Officer Alan Baribeau); p. **12** wheelsurf (www.wheelsurf.nl); Zuma Press pp. **5** (© Jose M. Osorio/Sacramento Bee), **20** (© Bandphoto/UPPA), **21** (© Bartlomiej Zborowski).

Cover photograph of the World Hovercraft Championships reproduced with permission of Getty Images (Stu Forster).

Every effort has been made to contact copyright holders of any material reproduced in this book. Any omissions will be rectified in subsequent printings if notice is given to the publisher.

Some words are shown in bold, **like this**. You can find out what they mean by looking in the glossary.

Contents

How Unusual!. 4

Pedaling Across the Sky 6

Tomorrow's Unicycle 8

The Monowheel. 10

By Land or by Sea 14

Blowing By 20

Art on Wheels. 22

Low Rider 24

Rocket Man 26

Test Yourself!. 28

Glossary 30

Find Out More 31

Index 32

How Unusual!

Have you ever seen something drive by that you couldn't believe? Maybe it was a car shaped like a hot dog. Maybe it was a truck that went underwater. Some of these weird machines do a special job. Others were just made for fun!

Why do you think these machines were built?

5

Pedaling Across the Sky

Want to fly and get some exercise at the same time? Try a **blimp** powered by pedaling. Hot air inside the blimp makes it float. The pedals turn a **propeller** that can make it go up to 12 mph (20 km/h).

EXTREME FACT

The driver of this blimp tried to pedal across the English Channel. But the wind blew him back!

Tomorrow's Unicycle

This small machine is a **unicycle** with a motor. The Honda U3X can move in any direction. You just lean your body. This is a good machine for moving inside. Just don't try to go down the stairs!

The Monowheel

Ever wonder what driving is like from a wheel's point of view? You can find out by riding a **monowheel**, which means "one wheel." Drivers sit inside the wheel. It can go more than 50 mph (80 km/h)!

EXTREME FACT

People thought up the
ideas for monowheels
back in the 1800s.

There are many different kinds of monowheels. The one below is powered by a motor. Others are pedaled like bikes. You turn them by leaning in one direction or another.

This monowheel is called the "Wheelsurf," because riding it feels like surfing on land!

By Land or by Sea

Some machines can go almost anywhere. **Amphibious** trucks can go on land or on sea. Some are used by the military. They can take people and equipment from a ship to the land. Or, they can attack a beach from the water. Then they drive onto the beach.

EXTREME FACT
Amphibious machines can drive right onto a ship!

항로봉

327

The Adventure Duck gives tours of China on land or sea.

Amphibious cars and trucks can be used for many things. Some give tours on land and water. Others are just driven for fun. Some cars and trucks can be **adapted** to use in water. But they need to be waterproof, and they need to float!

This machine is called the Surface **Orbiter**. Rick Dobbertin built it to drive over land and sea. He spent more than two years going halfway around the world!

The Surface Orbiter was built from a tank used to carry milk!

EXTREME FACT

You'll need **scuba gear** to drive this car. It can go as deep as 30 feet underwater! It was built without a roof so people could get out in an emergency.

Blowing By

A **hovercraft** drives on land or water. But it has no wheels, and it hardly even touches the ground! It uses fans to move around. A fan at the bottom blows into the ground. This keeps it "floating." Another fan in back pushes it forward.

These drivers are racing for the Hovercraft Championship.

Art on Wheels

Some unusual cars are made just to turn heads. They might be made to look like an object, such as a shoe or a dinosaur. Or they might be covered with something strange, such as grass.

↑ This scary car was created by artist William Burge. He named it "Phantoms."

This car is shaped like a dolphin!

23

Low Rider

A big car uses a lot of energy. But not this car! The Oxyride Racer is so small, you could walk over it. Being so low means the wind doesn't slow it down. It doesn't need much energy. It runs on store batteries!

You don't have much room in the Oxyride Racer!

Panasonic

Rocket Man

Yves Rossy wanted to fly without using an airplane. So he built a wing with a jet pack on it. He strapped it to his back and took off. Yves flew 22 miles across the English Channel. It took him only about 10 minutes!

EXTREME FACT

With wings on his back, Yves Rossy can go up to 186 miles per hour (300 km/h)!

Test Yourself!

Try to match up each question with the correct answer.

(1) Honda U3X

(2) Hovercraft

(3) Amphibious Machines

(4) Oxyride Racer

(5) Surface Orbiter

a Which machine is powered by batteries?

b Which machine is powered by fans?

c What military vehicles can go on land or water?

d Which machine moves when you lean forward?

e What was built from a tank used to carry milk?

Answers:
1 = d, 2 = b, 3 = c, 4 = a 5 = e

Glossary

adapted changed to use in another way

amphibious able to drive on land or in water

blimp vehicle that floats through the air

hovercraft machine that is powered by fans

monowheel machine with one wheel a that driver sits inside

orbiter a machine that goes around something, such as Earth

propeller spinning blade that pushes through air or water

scuba gear equipment that allows breathing underwater

unicycle cycle with only one wheel

Find Out More

Books

Kaelberer, Angie Peterson. *U.S. Marine Corps Assault Vehicles*. Mankato, MN: Capstone Press, 2007.

Sautter, Aaron. *Hovercraft*. Mankato, MN: Capstone Press, 2007.

Zuehlke, Jeffrey. *Concept Cars*. Minneapolis, MN: Lerner Publishing, 2007.

Websites

Nissan Pivo 2
http://www.nissan-global.com/EN/PIVO2/
Learn all about the Nissan Pivo 2.

More on Monowheels
http://www.roadsideresort.com/blog/the-future-of-travel-revealed-the-ginormous-wheel
See pictures and stories from this history of monowheels and unicycles.

Amphibious Machines and Hovercrafts
http://library.thinkquest.org/04oct/00450/index1.htm
Learn more about these machines in this site built by a class of 4th and 5th graders.

Find out

How fast can a hovercraft go?

Index

adaptations 16
amphibious machines 14,
    15, 16, 18, 19

batteries 24
blimps 6, 7

cars 4, 16, 19, 22, 23, 24

Dobbertin, Rick 18

fans 20

Honda U3X unicycle 8
hovercrafts 20, 21

jet packs 26, 27

military 14
monowheels 10, 11, 12
motors 8, 12

Oxyride Racer 24, 25

pedals 6, 7, 12
propellers 6

Rossy, Yves 26, 27

scuba gear 19
Surface Orbiter 18

trucks 4, 14, 15, 16

unicycles 8